TRANSMIGRATION SOLO

JOSEPH CERAVOLO

TRANSMIGRATION SOLO

THE TOOTHPASTE PRESS
West Branch, Iowa :: January, 1979

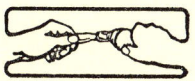

© 1979 by Joseph Ceravolo

No part of this book may be reproduced by any means, except for excerpts in critical articles, without written permission from author and publisher. Address all inquiries to:
The Toothpaste Press
Box 546 :: West Branch, Iowa 52358

C.I.P. Data

PS3553.E7T7   811'.5'4   79-1068
ISBN 0-915124-22-X   ISBN 0-915124-21-1 pbk.

This project was partially funded by the National Endowment for the Arts, and endorsed by the Iowa Arts Council. The publishers extend many thanks to these agencies.

CONTENTS

10 Lost Words
11 Life of Freedom
12 Sleep in Park
13 Descending the Slope
14 Feast of Visions
15 Floating Gardens
16 The Women
17 Lights of Childhood
18 Romance of Awakening
19 Invisible Autumn
20 Metaphorical Desert
22 Celebration
23 O Heart Uncovered
24 His Universe Eyes
25 Pain Songs
31 Migratory Noon
32 Contrast
33 Dinosaurs of Pain
34 Frozen Lookout
35 Stolen Away
36 Starting Up Again
37 White Sky
38 Chains of Mountains
39 Resting
40 Pastoral
41 Transmigration Solo
42 In Full View of Sappho
44 Spell of Eternity
45 Note from St. Francis

PREFACE

In the fall of 1960 I lived in the Colonia Ramos Millan, an outskirt of Mexico City. I had never felt as strong a connection between myself and a city. Nothing could move me from there. One day I saw Iztaccihuatl rising from luminous clouds more beautiful than light, and I wanted to climb it. I never did. Gradually I became homesick, smelling the leaves of the northeast, smelling an Autumn that wasn't there. By that time I had written the Mexican poems that appear in the first section of this volume with the exception of "Pain Songs," which was written in December 1960, in New York City, forgotten, lost, and rediscovered ten years later.

A group of poems from 1965 completes this volume of TRANSMIGRATION SOLO. Whether I chose them for contrast or for similarity of mood, I don't know, but I felt a brewing of diverse particles into the whole.

J.C.
1978

LOST WORDS

One corner is enough.
There isn't one
as the field bulbs go out.
Right nearby is a river.
Moon exhaustedness   slow (BIG)
slides lawns of earth under.
Moves paws, feet, nearby.
Closes this body in ground!

Is it Sunday? while throat of wind
swallows in the nest
the swallowable dark,
an incomplete you,
you so innocent —

> There's not enough words left,
> although it seems enough
> like grass inside me:
> where the moment
> is a terminable river
> and bush come home.

LIFE OF FREEDOM

Noise cells   Root barks   Piss grass,
The governments of tonight lay
like earthenware on sidewalks.
Arrange the geological brush, the wasp,
the part that makes it,
and out with a dog noise,
a night and the airplane lung.
The shadow on the wall
of multiple window mud-lamps
from street ceiling names that
sleep-bog their way across
a room of yesterdays,
of farms, of the interiors
of skins like
interiors of four o'clocks.

So as the park is,
where crust and piles of
yellow morning transfer
islandic barnacles to
leg trees, and wonderful
because it's cold,
your old feet in hand.
A big flower in park.
Onion life of freedom,
of green flies and lake,
of closest Spring and Fall.

SLEEP IN PARK

These, my understanding green,
and like tomorrow
along the Alameda,
the leather of your nights like
new departments of liquid
ride the syllable and come
between or after or inside.
What makes the afternoon
where funerals line the walls?
This is afternoon and a
tree is a house misunderstood
by the line-up on wall.
We follow standard judgement
and "no think", no brain
except what's under a brown
afternoon, and farther than
euclid rain slides across
the pillow which is clouds
of afternoon

DESCENDING THE SLOPE

I need a cliff I need zero
I need a cliff at 6:20,
and noise sounds thru pasty
soil of bus coughing
and spitting early morn fuel.
Think it's over? (the lights
coughing near sky . . . and
orange brown dispersion town).
There's the cliff,
there's the horrible cock
cracking his lungs
to the cliff.

Do you have guts?
Yes I have guts and a balloon.
We underestimate the whole process.
So what if there
are knots in wood.
They're smaller than all
the spots of rain, but
tomorrow we'll leave while
sky becomes poles of rain,
leave while clouds hounding
row stones regulate the scene .
The Michoacan river wheels
along the ropey scene,
and then it all ends:
tomorrow I mean

FEAST OF VISIONS

Instead it's that one damn spot
on the stained glass walls
of Mexico that looks like a man
wading his way in mud or water.

Seizure! blue wailing
questionaires of noonday
under the rotting trees.
Gracias mis amigos,
the river holds much mud
and he works for el gobierno
de Mexico
guarding trees,
riding a bicycle.
Oh mean women beating sheep,
sweep the dog shit
of three thousand dogs and niños
from your two foot sidewalks.
Tomorrow the fiesta
and mucho people
walk and see sun in river,
and cross over new
modern bridge made of pipes.

Ah, the dark eyes that
penetrate all the edificios
on the avenue.
The fiesta's fine, it
makes everyone think
that everything's just right.

FLOATING GARDENS

Sailing Sailing
under the creatura ridge,
and this less or more than obscure,
obsequious life follows the lives
of flies on beach.
"I'm happy", I said to big tree.

So we stand
on a ridge, it
has corners and we
wait in corners
of excellent summer,
unconscious manifolded igneous
summer,
and the flies on the pillow, sheet,
and cactus colored window
buzz the chandelier great white weather.
I'm far from a window.
Yet I am window and
feel the multicolored pushes
through open window self .

THE WOMEN

They have the corner
half seated on their thighs,
and long braids tied like drainpipes.
Their hair is a drainpipe
closed from rain.
In the corner of their eyes
is a building of grass.
Their smile cracks
plaster of paris streets.
When they look down
their eyes are orange slices.
They sell little peaches
with brown small rotten dots.

LIGHTS OF CHILDHOOD

You light like a flashlight
something through
the west of worn shades.
    All this great fun
    and you like a dark
    of misunderstanding only
    bring a large sample of green
    while people dance to
    rock and roll in spanish.
    All the littles on the wall watching
    while the parrot and dog again sleep.

The moon like a
stopped cannon ball:
so little difference between us.
I search the corners for you
and I am a drunk in a park
or a hallway at night.
Being in the street
is being gone in
the largest apple in universe

ROMANCE OF AWAKENING

Morning ground —
wet buildings light
my morning edifice group.
Animal, orange, mango, rat,
my weekday sleeping
as in a barn.
The rooster craps,
the most uncomfortable hour.
Brown instead. My lips!
are growing river brown.
Below — the house which departs
in open fields of round
      mechanicalness,
         melancholiness

INVISIBLE AUTUMN

The blade days ———
like Summer rush

Apollo leans.
The way the sun comes up,
the sun leans.
The sun leans less than
in the north, but one lean
is as good as another.
Now it's autumn, but
you would never know.

The blade days
like Summer, rush

METAPHORICAL DESERT

What do we do with
lemon nakedness desert arms
after ocean prying oneself?
This is synthetic day
clearly defined on the sleeves of evening
and how turned around
when rooster barks at six

We speak of the streets
and they become coordinative,
a fountain whose
water becomes a vein.
While light comes like
a moving overness,
a mosquito opera
we loose all (most of)
the scaryness of day.
Sure, what shakyness
in that these
aberrations are renounced.

If all, although only
the broken veins
of my tropical brothers,
through cloud sun atmosphere.
So and so will go
home or treeliness of age.
     Then along lugubrious ground,
sliding of hand, feet.

We've grown too much and
stayed along hedge perfumes
of the desert and walk
   in aberrations

CELEBRATION

The music is played. Play
the music
        O washable towns
Open wall   the wall
studio of moons,
Sell my bananas, I
mean buy my stones
of yellow obscure, of no
similarity. There are walls.
Something the same from nowhere rides. .
    Get off! there
are many fenders that
sound like some green place
without all this gravity.
The soft wind tonight ——
comes through trees
and river.
The town is people,
the people talk about town
about everything that isn't
town, that ends in people
and drizzle, that think
about a bottle and corn,
and some light on them
from the sweet sixteen party

O HEART UNCOVERED

We lived in province snow range
and something that we uncover
is like living
in one Arizona room
when we discover all we owe
to darkness
we never really know.

Tomorrow is the national holiday for independence —
no more left.
For the first time
we see the mountains
with snow on them pulling away
from the mountains and clouds.

HIS UNIVERSE EYES

Can we look through
this slanty night without getting dizzy,
and barking somewhere?
What was it about the first,
what wasn't it?

What kind?

    Whereat?

Then again the clouds
are bearable more than before.

We're invited to the river
by the river
and the wet flowers
that go along river
might not die again
           tonight.

PAIN SONGS

Back; gone country around,
like wind in hollow rabbit.
How many steps to take to
mud around, across,
Ixtapalapa green canal?
The cow is green, the
flax is brown; brown life
of flies, cool color, sickness, eyes.
Many over, what then?
There Jose stumbled on
market stands, dogs bit my clumsy foot.

Transport the ground, and
trees of olives like mouth
of understanding boulevards,
of green light mountains
where hills are filled with
lizards feet near home.
A silence as white as hospital clouds.

O breeze,
when I was young
and tried hard, when I was
there among 1000 footers,
off on off on the bird
on in, gone in in in flew.
Alone. The straw's
alone, the grave's alone,
the twitch, the switch,

the bitch's alone,
above clouds higher than moods.
It's late and the air's
as thin as straw,
and hill droves of relativity,
of hornet's hair sleep cool
as a quiet nosey rat.

Climbing up we passed it by,
maybe it was the cactus on
the knee or lizard in his pee.
It looked straight up as sun
boomed in rocks and big
zapilote bird made a shadow.

They asked me,
You going where in leaves?
Going when in road?
Sitting with all this sidewalk similarity.
It's like a bed unfolding
some high transportation of the street.
It is too much for street
here. How high it seems.

Pain, like blue is the
strap of night, the goulash
of darkness, a pool
of energy and green light signs;
signs of red, signs of night.
I leave, sandals fastened:
breeze warm as my hands, warm
as these warrior's hands.

I refuse, but accept that
if nothing else, there's
breath as thin as paper.

The path, the path is where?
It's the cow's, o but
to be near the cow.
Let's be near some old
realization that just died.
Near some depowdered
head that comes around
the horseshoe curves of sense.

But I discovered along the hedge
of waking that this
is me,
and around my skinniness I
place my clothes of disinterest,
and I bathe it, and
I bathe me anonymous.
I am unknown.
And in a rail-
road yard at dawn.

Biting a stick wondering
what it's all about under
the orange tree gloom bridge.
Let's count and
amount to everything we're
not supposed to.
That talk is from a young

brain, in a rebitten valley
of feathers, sky, beach,
sea, bush, volcano hump in the distance.

It's the sand perverse on
the boulevards that
swim Veracruzian desolation
in deep vocabulary afternoon:
a knot of sun comingles
the cactus, the sea, the plateau.

The day turns over on its
spine. Every faucet's
on. Ah! in the
haze, the grip running wall,
the sun grouping on the stillness
of your dark tide.
What sea gull blindness
on rocks, dunes, oil
pumps of your thoughts.
And the builders rinse their mouths and
the days of a week go swimming away.

There is a creek that passes.
It's a creek that
travels and looks like a bone,
within which all memory itself
has been.
There's no memory outside this.
There is only it.
I want the creek,

the feeling of its
depth like a body
on the fingers.

The morning awakes
and leaves me with one
hard thing. The summer
months sit on
a steeple (the only one around),
and the magnifying glass
of occupations leaves
the doors of a monsoon open,
growing from ridges of your lips.
You are young,
all roofs of world cannot
crush the highways of your newness.
When you're gone
it's as if someone
has taken away
the steps to a temple.

Wind is warm in the
store windows. It's November.
Surprise ducks leave a
canopy of a lake over the avenue.
To keep these secrets
we allay the nobody
seen on the cheeks of everyday.
Here! wear this spirit insignia.
Don't ask.
The line grows from yesterday.

Tomorrow it rained.
The light is mattress lipped,
and the pages born curtains.
Here! bang on my hand
frozen since Montezuma.
" Los pajaros ", not yet.
Whistle my breath
to the banging hammer hotel
and the Indian yellow blouse baby
carrying dirty serape beauty.
I listen
as I eat the street for supper,
listen to the pain songs
       of Mexico.
  Flashes of returning
  come with the birds.

MIGRATORY NOON

   Cold and the cranes.
Cranes in the
        wind
like cellophane tape
on a school book.
The wind bangs
the car, but I sing out loud,
      help, help
as sky gets white
  and whiter and whiter and whiter.
Where are you
  in the reincarnate
      blossoms of the cold?

CONTRAST

It's here in whatever shoots come up.
There's not a sound.
Like blossoms and grasshoppers
under the snow breathing little holes.
Is it death trying to see and breathe?
But I can't ask you to go.
        Do you understand?
What do you see?
The white snow,
the grey spears, oh grasshoppers,
        you rough grasshoppers
that are deader than a grasshopper
against my raw heart.

DINOSAURS OF PAIN

There are no dinosaurs
but man suffers still more.
>Morning, roaring
>tiger of trying to keep.

In the engine silo,
>there are no dinosaurs
>of pain that are hurried
>enough: Morning Star!

FROZEN LOOKOUT

Legs are cold.
    Beneath the knees   the legs
    are cold. The sun.
      The ball is out
   The ice is out.
Low.
The lips are warm
  beneath the knees.
  The ankles are cold; The tongue
  like a sweet dragon.
The ball   like
    dragon's eyes
  (I've never loved one)
   beneath the lashes like
    dragons' eyes
Refreshments Refreshments, no refreshments

STOLEN AWAY

How do people feel
               in this cold
    in this win...   win.... windy nest
    in the gloss like a
               cold nest
        in the tendon of life.

        The benches   feel
        like green alligators,
        crocodiles in the snow

I get
  a warm mouth
  on the hair
Someone has kissed me.
That boy and girl
fight and kiss in the car.
        A deep sound comes from it.
The birds fly down
    one by one, drop by drop.

STARTING UP AGAIN

What am I gonna do
    on this road? The sun drafting
    us. Nothing is
       brought beneath its own
       transmission. The stars
that are gonna come out soon.
Oh lively insects in
           the light. Criss-cross.

WHITE SKY

O sacred women going
        to work
            in the shallow, in the
                morning
in the brands of morning.
    Close my hand, open my
        hand against the wine.
The throat is dense and
    yellow.
It's only morning and the sun
        has become whiter
          forming on everything.

CHAINS OF MOUNTAINS

The clouds are panting.
There is a subequal brightness.
It makes my eyelids shake
in the morning submarine of leaves.
I think: where would my
dog be if I had one?
Like this brightness that's rubbed
in the morning.
And I touch this piece
       of metal and it is cool
cool as a morning swim.
But I hear no mountains.

RESTING

Oh bum!
there's nothing in a life
Oh dead
Oh dead
Oh yes
    The volcanoes in Tlacotal

PASTORAL

Regular quality. Drowsy in the sun
and now we've dressed.
    Good boy, let's go!

    I'll lie here in the park.
Guard me! I might be stabbed.
But only the grass stabs.
  With a dark creepy garden
enveloping my shirt
I am here, lonely and friendly.
Nursing like a baby
the instantaneous wind, the air
and the melt of the birds' cries:
    your play cries.

TRANSMIGRATION SOLO

See the black bird
in that tree
trying out the branches, puzzled.
I am up here with you
puzzled against the rain
blinking my eyes.

IN FULL VIEW OF SAPPHO

        Why are we
always fighting? Penetrate my heart!
      Bees are penetrating
    the hides of dead men.
Get some of that nameless life.
      Protect out young!
You beautiful and viscious
  God. Invisible and magical.
      You can't protect us.
  What are we?
  You have no power
  Doomed!   Lost!   Gone!

Returned! Lit up from loving
or from the absence of love.
     So invisible and
magical, playful and nameless.
        There is no power
except what you have.
Except what we have in our
playfulness toward you:
like bees in a space less hive.
Indian summer comes to us.

It begins the machine
of leaves falling and of bees
like little diving airplanes.

Even the heart of defecating men
 in carbon sorrow are candescent

voices of each other.
Where are we
alone? but with decaying
flowers that return and
    a falling love!
O climbing adrenalin of neverending
passion in winter!
A siren climbs through the air,
the children are yelling
outside. I am caught up
    in you, I admit it.
How different it all is.

SPELL OF ETERNITY

We are going to the park.
There are swings there.
There are rocks along a sand bed.
The flowers rest along
the bed. The flowers
rise among the fatigued
insects invading them.
There is a smell.
It invades us
through the insects
and makes us
notice there are flowers along
the bed, tiny flower clusters.
I envy the smell along the beds.
Is this a decaying soul? But
it is not said.
Am I decaying like
autumn insects, autumn leaves?
Find my heart!
Revive it! The old clouds
you find along the sky
have no chance next to you,
because it is autumn,
autumn.

NOTE FROM ST. FRANCIS

In the world today
there is
no world so attached as I am
to worlds.
All our hairyness
all our coarseness.
There is no texture in this
warmth I feel about
the creatures today.
We are gunning for extinction.
The sky is still bright
and all the animals running
for prehistoric sounds
believable in the passionate night.

COLOPHON

This book was designed by Cinda Kornblum. The Centaur type was handset by Allan Kornblum and printed on Strathmore Pastelle text. Of this first edition of of 1,100 copies, 100 were numbered and signed by the author, and handbound at the Black Oak Bindery; the remaining 1,000 were smyth sewn and glued into wrappers at the Laurance Press.